CHOCOLATE

Jacqueline Dineen

Illustrations by John Yates

Food

Apples	**Herbs and spices**
Beans and pulses	**Meat**
Bread	**Milk**
Butter	**Pasta**
Cakes and biscuits	**Potatoes**
Cheese	**Rice**
Chocolate	**Sugar**
Citrus fruit	**Tea**
Eggs	**Vegetables**
Fish	

All words that appear in **bold** are explained in the glossary on page 30.

Editor: Geraldine Purcell

First published in 1990 by Wayland (Publishers) Limited
61 Western Road, Hove, East Sussex BN3 1JD, England.

© Copyright 1990 Wayland (Publishers) Limited

British Library Cataloguing in Publication Data
Dineen, Jacqueline
  Chocolate.
  1. Chocolate
  I. Title II. Series
  641.3374

ISBN 0–7502–0046–4

Typeset by Kalligraphic Design Ltd., Horley, Surrey
Printed in Italy by G. Canale & C.S.p.A., Turin
Bound by Casterman S.A., Belgium

Contents

What is chocolate? 4

Chocolate in the past 6

Where does chocolate come from? 10

Growing cocoa trees 12

Harvesting the cocoa 14

From farm to factory 16

Making cocoa powder 18

Making chocolate 20

Chocolate and your body 22

Cooking with chocolate 24

Chocolate crispies 26

Brownies 27

Chocolate cake 28

Glossary 30

Books to read 31

Index 32

What is chocolate?

Anyone who has ever tasted chocolate knows that it is a delicious sweet food. How many foods made with chocolate can you think of? There are chocolate bars and boxes of chocolates with different centres. There are chocolate-covered sweets and biscuits, chocolate-flavoured cakes and puddings, and chocolate ice-cream. The chocolate itself may be the plain (dark) or the milk variety. Chocolate is popular all over the world and it is used in many different ways.

Do you know what chocolate is made from? Both types of chocolate start as beans growing in pods on cocoa trees. The dried beans are roasted and ground to make cocoa powder. You may have had hot cocoa in the evening before going to bed. Chocolate is made from **cocoa mass** with sugar and sometimes milk added to it.

Chocolate in the past

Cocoa trees grow wild in the **tropical** rain forests of South America. Hundreds of years ago, the Incas of Peru and the Aztecs of Mexico discovered that cocoa beans could be roasted to bring out the chocolate flavour. They crushed the roasted beans and mixed them with water, **vanilla** and spices to make a chocolate drink. The Aztec name for this drink was *Chocolatl*. That is where the name chocolate comes from.

Cocoa beans were so valuable that people

The meeting between Cortés and the Aztec emperor, Montezuma, in 1519.

used them as money. They would exchange beans for other things they needed, such as tools or cloth.

Spanish invaders, led by Hernando Cortés, arrived in Mexico in 1519. Cortés brought cocoa beans and a recipe for the chocolate drink back to Spain. The Spaniards kept their new discovery a secret for about 100 years. Then, Queen Marie

Thérèse of Spain introduced the drink to her husband, King Louis XIV of France. News of the delicious drink gradually spread. It reached England in about 1650, and the first chocolate drinking house opened in London in 1657. By the eighteenth century, there were several of these 'chocolate houses' where fashionable people could meet to drink chocolate and gossip.

Chocolate was very expensive because it had

Chocolate houses were popular places for people to meet and gossip during the seventeenth and eighteenth centuries.

Left Some chocolate products displayed in a shop window in France.

Below An advertisement for eating chocolate.

heavy **import duties**. It was a luxury that only rich people could afford. Smugglers began to bring cocoa beans into England and other countries in Europe **illegally**. The smuggled cocoa was sold more cheaply, so poorer people could afford to buy it. By 1850 it had become popular to eat chocolate as well as to drink it.

Today, people all over the world enjoy chocolate, though a box of chocolates is still a special treat!

Where does chocolate come from?

Until the end of the nineteenth century, all cocoa beans had to be shipped from South America. It was the only place where cocoa trees grew. In 1879, some young cocoa trees were planted in West Africa, where the **climate** was similar to South America. The trees flourished and by the early twentieth century, many farmers in West Africa were growing cocoa trees.

Today nearly half the world's cocoa beans are grown in the countries of West Africa. The main

Cocoa trees growing on the Caribbean island of Grenada.

10

Sacks of dried cocoa beans being loaded on to a ship at a dock in Brazil, ready to be exported.

producers are Ghana, the Ivory Coast and Cameroon. Cocoa beans are also grown in other parts of Africa, Central and South America, the West Indies and parts of Asia. Cocoa trees only grow in the tropical rain forest near the **equator** where there is hot sunshine and plenty of rain all year round.

About 2,000 tonnes of cocoa are produced each year. It is **exported** all over the world. The main **importers** are the USA and Europe.

Growing cocoa trees

Some cocoa trees are grown on large **plantations**. Others are grown on small farms.

Farmers plant the cocoa seeds in nursery beds and carefully look after the seedlings until they are two or three months old. They are then ready to be **transplanted**.

Above *This farmer, in Cameroon, takes care of the seedlings in his nursery.*

Opposite page *Young cocoa trees are being shaded by taller trees on this plantation in Malaysia.*

Cocoa trees like heat but they also need shade. Farmers may plant the seedlings near taller trees, such as coconut or banana trees. These provide food for the family as well as shade for the cocoa trees.

A fully-grown cocoa tree is 6–10m tall. It does not produce pods until it is four or five years old. Then, clusters of tiny flowers start to grow on the trunk and branches of the tree. The flowers produce small green pods called *cherelles*.

13

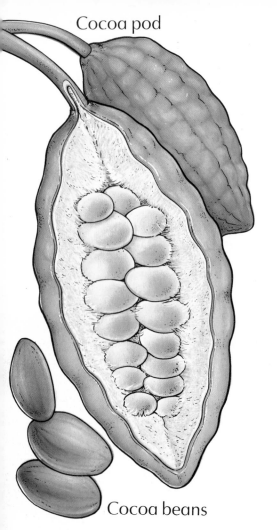

Cocoa pod

Cocoa beans

Harvesting the cocoa

The pods take about five months to grow and ripen. A ripened pod is 15–25 cm long and its colour changes from green to golden yellow.

The pods do not all ripen at the same time. It is very important to pick each pod at exactly the right moment. If one is picked before it is quite ripe, or left to fall off the tree, the beans inside

Right This Brazilian farmer is using a machete to harvest the ripe cocoa pods.

14

Left *An opened cocoa pod shows the beans and mucilage inside.*

Below *Cocoa pods ripen at different times.*

will not make such good cocoa. During the harvesting season, farmers check their cocoa trees regularly to find the ripe pods. They cut them from the tree using a long knife called a machete.

Farmers are helped by their families and workers from the local village. They pick the pods and carry them in baskets to a collection point. Each pod contains about 40 purple beans surrounded by a white pulp called mucilage. The pods are broken open with machetes so that the beans and pulp can be scooped out.

From farm to factory

This boy in Grenada is scooping out the insides of the harvested pods.

Cocoa beans taken straight from the pod taste bitter and not at all like chocolate. The beans have to be **fermented** to bring out the chocolate flavour. When the beans and pulp have been scooped out of the pods, they are heaped on to a layer of banana leaves. The heap is covered with more leaves and left for six days. The hot sun beats down and the temperature of the heap rises, which causes the beans to ferment. During fermentation, they turn from purple to brown.

When the beans have fermented, they are spread out on raised mats and left to dry for ten to twenty days.

When the beans are dry, the farmers and their workers put them into sacks which are then loaded on to lorries. They are taken to the local buying agent who buys cocoa for the

Left The cocoa beans are carefully spread out to dry in the sun.

Below A government buying agent checks and weighs the dried cocoa beans in Malaysia.

government from all the farmers in the area. Before paying the farmers, the agent weighs the beans and checks that they are good quality.

The sacks of beans are taken to a port and loaded on to a ship for export. They will be made into cocoa powder and chocolate in the countries that buy them.

Making cocoa powder

Drinking chocolate being served by an eighteenth-century Viennese waitress.

The ship docks at a port in the country which is buying the cocoa beans. The sacks are loaded on to lorries and taken to a cocoa factory.

At the factory, the beans are cleaned and then roasted in large ovens. Roasting gives the beans an even better chocolate flavour. The beans are then passed between rollers which crack the shells. Jets of air blow the bits of shell away from the centre or 'nib' of the bean. This process is called **winnowing**.

The nibs are put into another machine which grinds them into a liquid called cocoa mass. Half of the nib is **cocoa butter** which is too rich to be used in cocoa powder. To remove the cocoa butter, the mass is put into a press which squeezes it out. This cocoa butter can then be used in the production of chocolate.

The mass is made into round cakes which are cooled until they are solid. They are then put into a crushing mill to be ground into cocoa powder. The cocoa powder is packed into tins or packets, ready for the shops.

Cocoa powder is packaged before being sent to the shops.

Making chocolate

The mass for chocolate is made in the same way as it is for cocoa powder, except that all the cocoa butter is left in. To make plain chocolate, the mass is mixed with sugar and extra cocoa butter. Milk is added to make milk chocolate.

The ingredients are mixed together and then passed through rollers to make a smooth paste. The paste is put into a **conching** machine which blends the ingredients thoroughly. Conching takes three days for plain chocolate and slightly

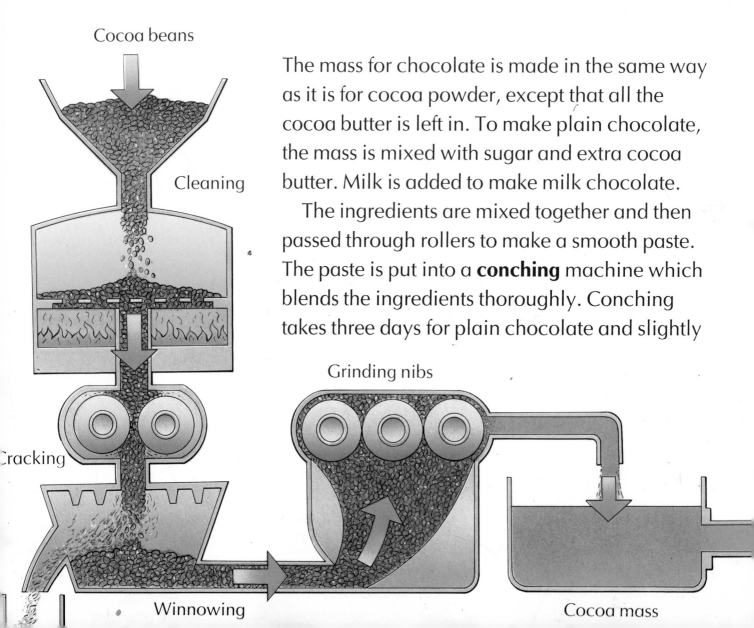

Cocoa beans

Cleaning

Cracking

Winnowing

Grinding nibs

Cocoa mass

less for milk chocolate.

Bars of chocolate are made by pouring liquid chocolate into moulds. The chocolate-filled moulds are cooled and the chocolate sets hard.

Liquid chocolate can also be poured over biscuits and sweets. Covering centres in this way is called 'enrobing'. Some chocolates are made by putting a centre into a mould with some chocolate already in it. More chocolate is then poured over to cover the centre.

When the chocolate products have cooled, they are wrapped or put into boxes before leaving the factory.

This diagram shows how chocolate is made.

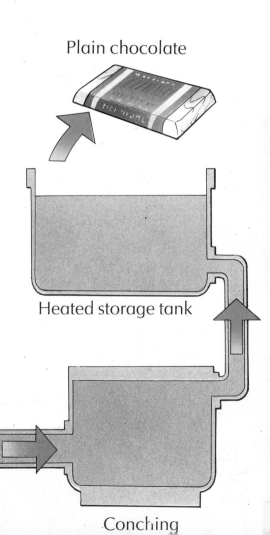

Plain chocolate

Heated storage tank

Sugar

Cocoa butter

Grinding

Conching

Chocolate and your body

Carbohydrates are foods which give us energy. Bread, potatoes and sugar are all carbohydrates. Chocolate contains sugar which the body can use to produce energy. Mountaineers, explorers and soldiers often carry chocolate in their **survival kits** to give them instant energy when they need it.

Chocolate is included in the Australian Army's survival kits.

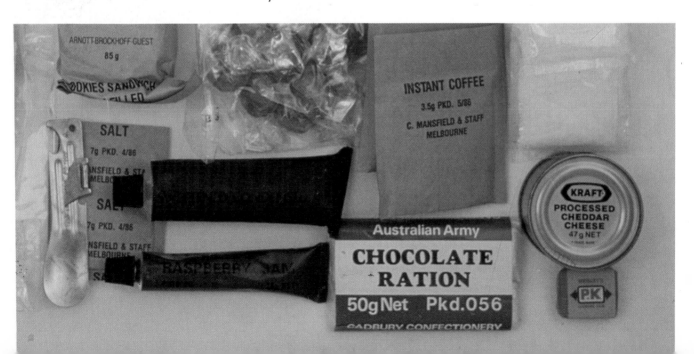

Chocolate can give people the energy to run or play sports. In the past, the London Marathon was sponsored by a chocolate manufacturer.

Carbohydrates can be fattening if you do not use up the energy by exercising. It is unhealthy to be overweight, so people have to watch how many carbohydrates they eat. Too much sugar also causes tooth decay. Brushing your teeth regularly helps stop tooth decay, but it is best not to eat too many sugary foods and sweets.

Cooking with chocolate

What sort of food do you have for your birthday parties? Do you have chocolate biscuits and cakes? Have you ever had a chocolate birthday cake? Chocolate is now an everyday food instead of the expensive luxury it once was, but it is still popular for special occasions. Cooks and chefs all over the world use chocolate to make delicious cakes and puddings, and to cover or

Above *Cooking with chocolate can be fun.*

Left *You can make delicious cake decorations from chocolate.*

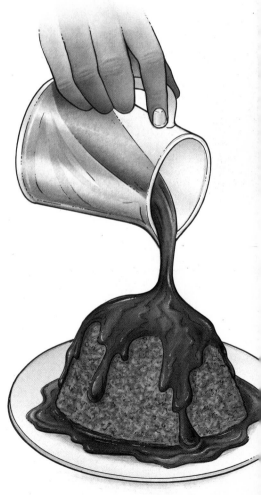

decorate a variety of foods.

Have you ever cooked with chocolate? As you already know, it melts when it is heated and hardens when it is cooled. This is not good if you are eating it on a hot day, but it is useful if you are cooking with it. You can melt it to pour over biscuits and puddings, or to make your own sweets. You can also mix it with icing sugar to ice cakes. Cocoa powder is also used to give a chocolate flavour to cakes and puddings.

Chocolate crispies

You will need:

100g plain chocolate

12g butter

75g cornflakes, or other non-sweetened breakfast cereal

margarine

2. Remove the bowl from the heat. Stir the cornflakes into the melted chocolate. Make sure all the flakes are coated.

1. Put the chocolate and butter in a bowl over a saucepan of hot water. Stir until the chocolate melts.

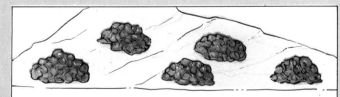

3. Coat some greaseproof paper with margarine to stop the mixture from sticking.

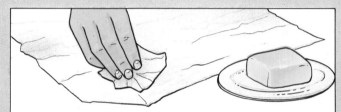

4. Pile the mixture in small heaps on the greaseproof paper. Leave in a cool place until the chocolate has set.

Brownies

You will need:

100g butter
100g plain chocolate, broken into pieces
100g soft brown sugar
100g self-raising flour
a pinch of salt
2 eggs, beaten
50g walnuts, chopped
1–2 tablespoons milk

These are very popular in the USA.

1. Put the butter and chocolate into a bowl over a saucepan of hot water. Stir until melted. Remove the bowl from the heat and stir in the sugar. Mix thoroughly and leave to cool.

2. Sieve the flour and salt into a mixing bowl. Make a well (a hollow) in the centre and pour in the chocolate mixture. Mix together.

3. Add the eggs and walnuts. Stir the milk in to the mixture.

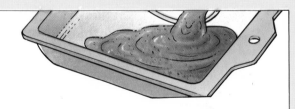

4. Grease a 20cm square cake tin and pour the mixture in. Bake in the centre of the oven at 180°C/350°F/gas mark 4 for about 30 minutes. Leave to cool then cut into squares.

Chocolate cake

You will need:

150g self-raising flour
½ level teaspoon cream of tartar
½ level teaspoon salt
200g caster sugar
100g margarine
150ml milk
1 teaspoon vanilla essence
2 eggs
50g plain chocolate, melted

2. Sieve the flour, cream of tartar and salt into a bowl. Add the sugar, margarine, milk and vanilla essence. Mix together and beat well for two minutes. Add the eggs and chocolate. Beat for one minute.

1. Grease a 17.5cm round cake tin with a bit of margarine. Make a circle of greased greaseproof paper to line the bottom of the tin.

3. Pour the mixture into the tin. Bake in the centre of the oven at 180°C/350°F/gas mark 4 for about 1¼ hours.

For the filling:

100g butter
225g icing sugar
100g plain chocolate
1 tablespoon milk

5. Break the chocolate into pieces. Put the chocolate and milk into a bowl and melt over a pan of hot water. Make sure an adult helps you with this bit. Then stir the chocolate into the butter and icing sugar.

4. Beat the butter until it is light and fluffy. Sieve the icing sugar and add to the mixture.

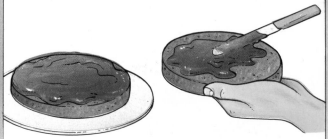

6. Cut the cake into two layers. Spread some of the icing mixture on each layer and press them together. Spread the rest of the mixture on top of the cake.

Glossary

Carbohydrates Energy-giving substances found in foods such as sugar, bread and potatoes.

Climate The usual weather conditions of a region.

Cocoa butter The fatty substance in a cocoa bean.

Cocoa mass The liquid made from grinding the nibs of the cocoa bean together.

Conching The process of stirring liquid chocolate until it becomes a smooth mixture.

Equator The imaginary line around the middle of the Earth.

Exported When goods are sent to be sold in another country.

Fermented When a substance has been broken down by a chemical change through heat, moisture or an added ingredient.

Illegally Acting against the law.

Import duties Extra payments charged on goods being brought into a country.

Importers People who buy goods from another country.

Plantations Large areas of land where one type of crop is grown.

Survival kits Contain food and equipment which help people to survive in emergencies.

Transplanted When young plants are taken up and replanted somewhere else.

Tropical The very hot and rainy climate near the equator.

Vanilla The flavouring that comes from a variety of orchid.

Winnowing The separating of grain or seed from the husk or shell by air blowing the lighter parts away.

Books to read

Milk by Dorothy Turner (Wayland, 1988)

Focus on Cocoa by Graham Rickard (Wayland, 1988)

The Food We Eat by Jennifer Cochrane (MacDonald, 1975)

Index

Africa 11
Asia 11
Australia 22

Brazil 11, 14

Cameroon 11, 13
Carbohydrates 22–23
Central America 11
Chocolate
  bars 4, 9, 21
  biscuits 4, 21, 24–25
  boxes 4, 9, 21
  cakes 4, 21
  drink 6–9, 18–19
  health 22–23
  icing 25
  making 20–21
  milk 5, 20
  plain 5, 20
  puddings 4, 25
  sweets 4, 21, 25
'Chocolate houses' 8

Cocoa
  beans 5–7, 10, 14–18
  butter 18, 20
  growing 12–13
  mass 5, 18–19
  pods 5, 10, 13–16
  powder 5, 18–19
  seedlings 12–13
  trees 5–6, 10–15

England 8–9
Equator 11
Europe 9, 11

Factory 18–19
Fermenting beans 16
Flavouring 4, 25
France 8, 9

Ghana 11
Grenada 10, 15, 16

Harvesting 14–15

Ivory Coast 11

Malaysia 12, 17
Mexico 6, 7

Nursery plants 12–13

Peru 6
Plantations 12

Roasting beans 5, 6, 18

South America 6, 10, 11
Spain 7, 8

Transplanting trees 12
Tropical rain forests 6, 11

USA 11

West Africa 10, 11
West Indies 11

Picture acknowledgements

The photographs in this book were provided by: Cadbury's Ltd 6, 9 (right), 17 (left), 19; Hutchison 10, 13, 15, 16; Mary Evans Picture Library 7 (both), 18; Christine Osborne 12, 17 (right); Peter Stiles COVER; Topham Picture Library 9 (left), 15 (left), 22, 23, 24, 25; WPL 8; ZEFA 11, 14.